Salesforce

Introduction: Build value, reduce anxiety, and advance your Salesforce career

Koso Brown

Copyright 2024© Koso Brown

All rights reserved. This book is copyrighted and no part of it may be reproduced, distributed, or transmitted in any form or by any means, including photocopying, recording, or other electronic or mechanical methods, without the prior written permission of the publisher, except in the case of brief quotations embodied in critical reviews and certain other non-commercial uses permitted by copyright law.

Printed in the United States of America
Copyright 2024© Koso Brown

Contents

Introduction 1

Chapter 1 2

What is Salesforce? 2

Chapter 2 9

Acquiring and Presenting Competencies 9

Chapter 3 15

Salesforce's Architecture 15

Chapter 4 21

Choosing a Career Path within the Salesforce Ecosystem 21

Chapter 5 26

Adapting to New Features and Technologies to Stay Ahead 26

Chapter 6 30

Handling the Salesforce Employment Market Insider Job Hunting Techniques 30

Chapter 7 34

Proven Real-World Examples of The Advantages of Salesforce Experiences 34

Conclusion 46

Introduction

Do you recall when phone conversations were used to handle customer interactions and all customer data was kept in physical files? The on-premise CRM software, which had large upfront expenditures, restricted scalability, and no automation, restricted the potential of enterprises. Due to these issues, cloud-based CRMs, such as Salesforce, were developed to assist organizations in managing their customer interactions.

You are about to learn about Salesforce, the top cloud-based CRM in the world, through this reading. We will take you through Salesforce's definition, operation, business benefits, and available cloud options.

Are you prepared to find out more? Now let's get started.

Chapter 1

What is Salesforce?

Allow me to begin by defining. Salesforce is an online program that users can access. The company provides cloud-based software as a service (SaaS). Pay-as-you-go subscriptions are the basis of its business strategy. Salesforce is always accessible from any device because all its data and information are kept on cloud servers. Moreover, accurate real-time updates and live data tracking are made possible.

In short, Salesforce is a customer relationship management (CRM) specialist. This is how it functions. It should come as no surprise that a CRM platform aids businesses in improving their interactions with both present and new clients.

The technology can determine who the top leads in an organization are and can even recommend actions and next steps. Salesforce's features go beyond attracting new clients; they are designed to maintain existing clients, which fosters brand loyalty.

Although there are other CRMs available, Salesforce is quickly taking the lead in the sector. It provides a wide range of services that let companies interact with their clients in more meaningful ways than just surface-level interactions

What is the purpose of the Salesforce CRM system?

It aids companies in boosting sales.

Salesforce increases earnings for businesses by assisting them in expanding their sales teams and generating more revenue.

Here are some more precise numbers, as you are already familiar with the Salesforce explanation. Today, Salesforce serves over 150,000 businesses, including T-Mobile, Aetna Health, Carvana, and Adidas, with their CRM requirements. It bills itself as a pathfinder and has numerous innovative features that add up to a substantial value.

The benefit of Salesforce eCommerce integration is that it gives businesses a comprehensive understanding of their clientele. Businesses can market more strategically thanks to the platform's features, which enable them to convert prospects into customers and foster loyalty.

Moreover, it facilitates team management by coordinating service, sales, and marketing to keep everyone in sync. Salesforce brags about its sophisticated algorithm that produces more productive agents.

From a customer service perspective, Salesforce enables businesses to address customer support concerns more quickly. The platform's helpful analytics data is crucial in driving future marketing initiatives and boosting income streams for the business.

It assists companies in monitoring their relationships with customers.

Salesforce can assist companies that offer goods or services in tracking their sales prospects.

It aids companies in managing their sales prospects.
Following up on sales prospects can be a full-time workload. Salesforce gives companies a location to store all of their customer and sales data, which makes it easier for them to keep track of their sales prospects.

It aids companies in managing client information.
Salesforce provides a plethora of capabilities to assist companies in expanding their sales teams and boosting profits.

How Is Salesforce Operational?
Salesforce is a cloud-based CRM system that gives your teams access to all the customer data they require across all departments. What is the purpose of Salesforce in this instance? In this case, it serves to

establish a bond amongst team members, enabling them to improve customer experience and boost revenue for your business.

Let's have a look at a Salesforce sample. CRM is used by the marketing department to plan and analyze promotions, advertisements, and other consumer interactions. The data can be viewed by the IT and finance departments, who can then modify your system accordingly. The ultimate purpose of all of this is to increase your company's profitability.

Characteristics of Salesforce adoption by industries and companies, along with career opportunities

Salesforce is becoming the preferred CRM solution for many businesses and organizations. Salesforce has shown to be a flexible platform able to meet a variety of corporate demands, from finance and healthcare to retail and non-profit. As a result, Salesforce workers have a wide range of demanding and interesting job options in these areas.

- ❖ **Non-profit:** To track fundraising efforts, manage donor connections, and promote community engagement, non-profit organizations are implementing Salesforce. Volunteer coordinators, program managers, and development officers are just a few non-profit roles using Salesforce.
- ❖ **Retail:** Stores are using Salesforce to monitor consumer preferences, improve advertising campaigns, and offer tailored in-store experiences. A variety of Salesforce positions are available in the retail industry, such as CRM administrators, e-commerce experts, and retail application developers.

- ❖ **Healthcare:** As the emphasis on patient care and engagement grows, Salesforce is being used by healthcare organizations to handle patient data more effectively, collaborate more effectively, and provide more individualized treatment. Opportunities for employment in this industry include consultant, developer, and Salesforce administration positions

❖ **Finance:** To increase customer happiness, expedite sales procedures, and adhere to legal requirements, financial institutions are using Salesforce. Careers at Salesforce in finance are available in various sectors, including banking, insurance, wealth management, and financial technology.

Salesforce will give you lots of chances to positively impact organizations and contribute to their success, regardless of the sector or company you work for.

Skills & Requirements for Careers at Salesforce

A Salesforce profession requires a variety of credentials, certifications, and abilities, some of which are necessary for specific roles. This is a summary of the requirements for success whether you want to work as a consultant, administrator, or developer with Salesforce.

Chapter 2

Acquiring and Presenting Competencies

Projects and experience are essential for developing and exhibiting the abilities required for a Salesforce career. Make the most of opportunities to work on real-world initiatives, whether they come from personal projects, internships, or volunteer work. You may hone your technical skills, show off your problem-solving prowess, and build a portfolio of effective solutions with this practical experience.

Consider getting certified in Salesforce as well. These credentials attest to your proficiency in particular fields, which increases your value to companies. Numerous certifications are available from Salesforce, such as those for Administrator, Developer, Consultant, and more. Obtaining these credentials can greatly increase your credibility and lead to new professional prospects.

Add projects, certifications, and experience to your LinkedIn profile, online portfolio, and resume. In the competitive Salesforce employment market, this helps you distinguish yourself from other candidates by showcasing your abilities and accomplishments.

Keep in mind that a Salesforce career demands both technical and soft abilities. Develop and hone these abilities constantly to succeed in the changing Salesforce ecosystem.

Soft Skills

Soft skills are just as crucial for success in Salesforce professions as technical skills. Since you will frequently be collaborating with cross-functional teams to gather requirements and provide solutions to stakeholders, communication is essential. Effective and transparent communication is essential for productive teamwork and mutual understanding.

Another essential ability is the ability to solve problems. Salesforce specialists frequently encounter challenging business problems, and they are required to devise creative solutions. Having an analytical and rational perspective will help you succeed as you work through different assignments and projects.

Technical Proficiency

Technical proficiency is essential for Salesforce jobs. Skills in Apex, Visualforce, and Lightning are frequently needed for professions involving development and customization. With these abilities, you can develop dependable apps, streamline corporate procedures, and design aesthetically pleasing user interfaces.

It's also critical to have a solid grasp of the Salesforce platform's capabilities and constraints. This information aids in the decision-making process during solution design, guaranteeing optimum performance and scalability.

Why is Salesforce applied?

With the help of Salesforce, businesses of all sizes and sectors can expand their clientele and gain a greater understanding of their clients. To allow employees to exchange client views from any device, regardless o department or location, businesses usually integrate Salesforce into their ecosystem.

With its streamlined workflows, consolidated cloud-based data management, and real-time tracking of customer statistics, Salesforce offers a 360-degree picture of the customer lifecycle. Salesforce claims that more than 150,000 enterprises, ranging in size from startups to Fortune 500 firms, make use of its safe and expandable cloud platform.

For instance, Pardot, a Salesforce business-to-business (B2B) marketing automation tool, was renamed Marketing Cloud Account Engagement in April 2022. Its functions include helping businesses track campaign performance, generate high-quality leads with potent marketing tools, automate lead qualification and nurturing, and improve sales acceleration.

How do cloud services and Salesforce interact?
Salesforce provides a variety of cloud platforms for certain specific uses. To briefly respond to the

question, "What does Salesforce do?"

- ❖ A system designed specifically for the healthcare sector, Salesforce Health Cloud aids clinics and hospitals in improving patient outcomes and operational effectiveness.
- ❖ Businesses may interact with customers at the appropriate times and through the appropriate channels by using the Marketing Cloud. Based on each user's unique interests, online habits, and other information, the platform customizes content for them individually. The information may come from a person's interactions on social media, their shopping habits, and more.
- ❖ The Analytics Cloud, also known as Einstein Sales Analytics, facilitates data interaction for enterprises, leading to increased transaction closings. Simple features for data visualization enable businesses to monitor team performance, identify patterns, act on opportunities, and more.

- ❖ Resources for customer service, marketing, and sales are all included in the Sales Cloud. It makes it possible for companies to offer tailored purchasing experiences to clients in B2B and B2C scenarios alike.

Chapter 3

Salesforce's Architecture

Salesforce's framework is its architecture. This framework serves as the foundation for all of its platforms, services, and applications. These programs offer the framework that powers Salesforce's operations. Because of its scalable architecture, Salesforce can adapt to the demands of many industries. It consists of:

Apps and Platform

Applications ranging from customer relationship management (CRM) to enterprise resource planning (ERP) are run on the platform at the heart of Salesforce's design. It might include cloud services designed expressly for various business needs, such as Sales Cloud, Service Cloud, Marketing Cloud, Commerce Cloud, Community Cloud, and Platform Cloud.

Data Model

The Salesforce architecture offers adaptable and configurable data model support. This implies that setups within Salesforce can be made to reflect field data, relationship settings, and object definition. Salesforce's architecture is robust because of its customizability, which enables businesses to adapt the platforms to suit their business procedures.

Integration Skills

To safeguard data and follow industry standards, Salesforce's architecture tightly incorporates security and compliance requirements into its design. Salesforce has implemented cutting-edge security features, such as encryption, access limits, and frequent security updates, among others, to protect data. Additionally, the platform supports a wide range of compliance standards that businesses can employ within the regulatory framework of their sector.

Safety and Adherence

Salesforce's architecture places a strong emphasis on security and compliance, with the platform built to safeguard data and guarantee adherence to industry norms. To protect data, Salesforce uses cutting-edge security methods including encryption, access limits, and frequent security updates. Furthermore, the platform is compatible with multiple compliance standards, guaranteeing that businesses may function within the established legal and regulatory parameters in their sector.

Interface User

A key component of Salesforce's architecture is the user interface, which is designed to make using the system simple for users. Salesforce apps are compatible with multiple devices, including tablets, smartphones, laptops, and desktop computers, enabling users to access them from any location. Usability, therefore, is one of Salesforce's architecture's main advantages since it boosts productivity and user satisfaction.

In conclusion, Salesforce's architecture is a thorough structure made to accommodate a variety of company processes, guaranteeing that businesses may use Salesforce to boost productivity, strengthen client relationships, and accomplish their objectives. Salesforce's architecture helps businesses succeed by offering a secure, flexible, and scalable platform.

Salesforce's Infrastructure

The foundation of Salesforce's architecture, which allows for the platform's scalability, dependability, and adaptability, is its infrastructure. Salesforce's infrastructure, which is hosted in the cloud and is extremely efficient and secure, guarantees that the platform can meet the needs of a variety of businesses, from start-ups to major corporations. This cloud-based method has several significant benefits:

Security

Security is the primary consideration in the architecture of Salesforce's cloud infrastructure. The platform uses cutting-edge security features to safeguard data and guarantee adherence to industry standards, such as encryption, access limits, and frequent security upgrades.

Dependability

Salesforce is hosted in the cloud, guaranteeing constant availability and accessibility to the platform. This lowers the possibility of downtime, which can be especially important for companies whose operations depend on Salesforce.

Adaptability

Salesforce can promptly adjust to changes in technological and business requirements thanks to its cloud-based architecture. This implies that consumers won't need to update their gear or software for Salesforce to roll out new features and enhancements.

Scalability

Organizations may effortlessly scale their Salesforce deployment up or down to their demands thanks to Salesforce's cloud architecture. This implies that Salesforce can handle rising demand as a company expands without necessitating a big initial investment in gear or software.

Maintenance and modifications

Organizations can take advantage of routine

upgrades and maintenance without having to handle their IT infrastructure because Salesforce maintains the infrastructure. This enables Salesforce to maintain the platform's security, functionality, and performance optimization.

In conclusion, a crucial part of Salesforce's architecture is its cloud-based infrastructure, which offers the scalability, dependability, and flexibility required to support the variety of business operations that Salesforce makes possible. Salesforce guarantees that businesses may effectively and securely use Salesforce to propel their commercial performance by utilizing the cloud.

Chapter 4

Choosing a Career Path within the Salesforce Ecosystem

Understanding the Salesforce Career Landscape

Starting a career with Salesforce is like putting your boat in a wide ocean of possibilities. The Salesforce ecosystem is a vibrant, ever-growing universe full of opportunities for a wide range of interests and skill sets. The career options are as varied as they are fulfilling, ranging from marketers and consultants to administrators and developers.

A map and compass are necessary for navigating this terrain; the first step is figuring out where you are and where you want to go. Here are some important checkpoints to think about along the way:

❖ **Strategy and Consultancy:** Consulting positions allow individuals with a combination of business and technical expertise to bridge the gap between the two.

- ❖ **The Career Path for Salesforce Admins:** It establishes the groundwork for comprehending the platform and is frequently the entry point into the ecosystem.

Explore specializations with distinct difficulties and benefits, such as Marketing Cloud, Sales Cloud, or Service Cloud.

Finding Your Specialization: Marketing Cloud Expertise

Finding your niche in the wide sea of Salesforce is like finding a beacon that directs your professional path. Becoming an invaluable member of any marketing team is the goal of Marketing Cloud Mastery, which goes beyond simply comprehending the platform. To do this, think about taking the following actions:

- ❖ Keep up with the latest innovations in technology and services that are changing the marketing landscape inside the Salesforce ecosystem.

- ❖ Explore all of Marketing Cloud Engagement's features and see how Salesforce's best practices are used to meet business needs.
- ❖ Obtain credentials that attest to your proficiency, such as Marketing Cloud Developer or Email Specialist.

You may put yourself at the forefront of marketing innovation and be prepared to take advantage of cutting-edge features and technologies that propel business success by concentrating on Marketing Cloud.

Always keep in mind that creating a strong CV is essential, and highlighting your expertise as a Salesforce Marketing Cloud Developer can help you stand out. If you grasp the fundamentals, such as finding solutions for local or corporate account structures, you'll be well on your way to being a highly sought-after authority in your industry.

Developing a Personal Development Plan and Identifying Career Goals

A job in the Salesforce ecosystem necessitates a dedication to ongoing personal and professional development, in addition to technical proficiency. The foundation of any successful development plan is the establishment of measurable, incremental targets. These objectives ought to be in line with both your own ambitions and industry norms to provide a positive feedback loop that keeps you motivated and successful.

- ❖ Establish Specific Objectives: Clearly state your objectives, such as obtaining a particular certification or becoming an expert in a particular Salesforce feature.

- ❖ Frequent pauses: To keep attention and avoid burnout, incorporate regular pauses into your schedule.
- ❖ Milestones: To maintain motivation, set aside time to acknowledge and appreciate every accomplishment, no matter how tiny.

- ❖ Connect with Peers: Make connections with other Salesforce experts to exchange experiences and learn fresh perspectives.

Incorporating innovative, disciplined, and forward-thinking techniques into your professional ethos not only helps you develop your career but also sets new standards for the industry. The only thing limiting your trajectory is how much you are willing to invest in strategic learning. With great enthusiasm, embrace this trip and see your career reach previously unheard-of heights.

Chapter 5

Adapting to New Features and Technologies to Stay Ahead

Those who want to succeed in the always-changing Salesforce landscape should embrace new features and technologies; it's not just a tip. The Salesforce ecosystem is ever-changing, with regular changes that have the power to alter the scene completely. One needs to be proactive and alert to stay ahead. You may put yourself at the forefront of innovation by choosing your learning resources carefully and looking to connect with industry leaders in sales.

By taking a proactive approach to learning, you can ensure that you have insights into upcoming trends and existing best practices. The following typical traps should be avoided:

- ❖ Ignoring the Basics: Before moving on to more complex modules, make sure you have a solid understanding of the basics.

- ❖ Not Doing Enough Practice: To solidify theoretical information, practical experience is essential.
- ❖ Ignoring Updates: To prevent obsolescence, it is essential to stay current with regular updates.

By implementing cutting-edge tactics, you become a trailblazer who breaks new ground in terms of success. The path leads to outstanding performance and a recognized career in the Salesforce ecosystem, and it is both difficult and incredibly rewarding.

Creating a Portfolio to Highlight Your Skills

Your portfolio serves as your storybook in the context of Salesforce Marketing Cloud development, chronicling your path through completed projects and accomplishments. It takes art to create a portfolio that appeals to prospective employers. It's important to create a narrative that showcases your abilities, originality, and influence rather than just reiterating the tasks you've completed.

- ❖ Emphasize Relevant Experience: Give specifics on the automated workflows you've built, the campaigns you've created, and the integrations you've mastered. Mention the platforms and tools you enjoy using, including Automation Studio, Journey Builder, and Marketing Cloud.
- ❖ Customize Your Content: Make sure your portfolio reflects the position you're applying for. Employ keywords from job descriptions to demonstrate the skills that employers are looking for.
- ❖ Measure Your Influence: Give specific figures. Did your efforts result in a 30% increase in conversions or a 20% rise in open rates? These numbers provide a powerful narrative about your worth.

More than just a collection of works, your portfolio serves as a guide for upcoming opportunities and a record of your professional development.

Recall that a well-designed portfolio displays not only

your technical proficiency but also your capacity for strategic thought and problem-solving. It's a venue where your prior achievements set the stage for future achievement.

Chapter 6

Handling the Salesforce Employment Market

Insider Job Hunting Techniques

While starting a job search inside the Salesforce ecosystem may seem intimidating, you can go through this process with confidence if you have the correct techniques. Networking is essential; it's more important to know who you know than what you know. Create connections with the community by participating in forums, social media, and Salesforce events; these connections may result in employment prospects.

- ❖ Examine the businesses that pique your attention, then adjust your strategy to meet their requirements.
- ❖ Maintaining current and sharp abilities is essential to standing out in a crowded market.

- ❖ Rehearse your interview techniques while concentrating on how you may benefit a prospective company.
- ❖ Recall that perseverance is essential. The Salesforce employment market is ever-changing, and chances may present themselves at any time. Remain aggressive, continue to hone your brand, and don't be scared to get in touch with recruiters or hiring managers directly.

How to Write a Resume That Gets You Hired

Your CV serves as the recruiting manager's compass when it comes to Salesforce careers. It's an art form to create a CV that speaks to your target audience; it takes a combination of planning, accuracy, and personality. To make sure your resume not only looks good but also attracts attention from potential employers, follow these steps:

- ❖ Include Useful Keywords: Make sure the language on your resume corresponds to the job description. This customized strategy directly addresses the requirements of the company and the particulars of the position.

❖ Display Your Projects: To provide a concrete example of your abilities, provide links to your portfolio or your contributions to open-source Marketing Cloud projects.

❖ Quantify Your Impact: Make use of indicators, such as higher open rates or conversion rates, to demonstrate the success of your marketing activities.

Recall that your CV tells the story of your career development. It should skillfully combine your technical expertise with anecdotes of your triumphs and obstacles faced. Create a resume that presents you as a developer who is not just well-versed in the Salesforce Marketing Cloud but also knows how to use it to create effective marketing campaigns. Not only should experiences and talents be listed on a CV, but they should also show how those attributes have produced outcomes and enhanced the success of previous projects.

When you polish your resume, think of it as your own

personal sales brochure, showcasing your best qualities and enticing prospective employers to find out more about the kind of person you would be a valuable asset to their company

Chapter 7

Proven Real-World Examples of The Advantages of Salesforce Experiences

1. **Engage in your community directly.**

   Organizations are increasingly asking their constituents for input on the services they are receiving as a result of the sector's heightened emphasis on accountability and transparency. With Salesforce Experiences, businesses can revolutionize community outreach and create new avenues for interaction and cooperation. It offers a single location where community members can go to obtain answers on their own, at their own pace, without having to communicate through protracted email threads, forms, or attachments. Members can set up "profiles" on a community portal, where they can update their progress, contact details, status, and more.

Whether you use Salesforce Experience Cloud as a forum, knowledge base, or self-service portal, allowing users to update their information can reduce the amount of extra email correspondence and establish a single source of truth for member information, saving your company time and hassles.

Global Health Corps

The goal of the Global Health Corps (GHC) is to organize a varied group of leaders to advance the cause of health fairness. For young professionals from a variety of backgrounds, GHC offers a 13-month paid fellowship that allows them to work with GHC's partners on the front lines of global health, develop their leadership abilities through transformative programming, and join a close-knit network that will support them throughout their careers.

Even though GHC has been using Salesforce for donor administration and fundraising since 2016, they lacked an easy-to-use, dependable method for staff to interact directly with the community and for fellows and alumni to exchange information. Built on Salesforce Experiences Cloud, GHC launched a Community Portal in 2017 that lets fellows and graduates establish personalized user profiles, look for members using filter criteria, and connect with peers in related groups.

GHC staff members have been sharing materials with fellows and alumni through the Community Portal for over three years. These resources include country information packs, travel guides, and fellowship policies. Users have access to a directory tool that lets them look for community members based on a variety of criteria. For instance, they can look for all Malawian users who have experience with HIV.

2. **Improve accountability and openness**
   Giving data to those who need it is part of our aim as a social enterprise to promote transparency in the social sector. This is particularly helpful for stakeholders who are making important decisions that ultimately

impact all of the important stakeholders in an organization, including beneficiaries, such as trustees and board members. Key external stakeholders (directors, trustees, reviewers) have access to Salesforce Experience Cloud to view, change, and comment on pertinent data.

3. **Reduce the workload associated with reporting**

Reporting procedures frequently result in hassles and the waste of time, which is our most precious resource. To free themselves and their partners/grantees up to concentrate on accomplishing their missions rather than entering data into spreadsheets, our clients frequently search for methods to reduce the reporting load.

Salesforce Experience Cloud facilitates the transition of data from email or form-based submission to a collaborative, continuous process within a shared Salesforce Experience Cloud workspace, thereby streamlining and strengthening reporting for our clients.

Experience Cloud, when combined with Amp Impact, can also help grantees and funders work together. It gives grantees access to a portal where they can monitor grant and disbursement progress, get in touch with other grantees, and submit impact, financial, and narrative reports.

The Global Good Fund

A nonprofit social company called the Global Good Fund (GGF) finds high-potential leaders who could have a bigger social effect if they had access to funding, professional leadership coaching, and executive mentorship. More than 160 entrepreneurs have been nurtured by the GGF Fellowship since 2013, and they are currently expanding their businesses faster in more than 40 countries.

For their yearly Fellowship Program, GGF and Vera Solutions started building a database in December 2018 to centralize fellow management and reporting tasks. By using Amp Impact to measure program impact, the system enables GGF to monitor fellow outcomes through dashboards and reports, track and report on baseline and final values for fellows' performance indicators, and offer a system that encourages consistency and ease in data entry and performance tracking.

Through the integration of GGF's Amp Impact-based system with Salesforce Experience Cloud, GGF Fellows may report directly on their budget and expenditure, as well as their goals for leadership development and indicator results. Afterward, using the Salesforce "Chatter Feed" in the Fellow Community, GGF personnel can examine these numbers and give fellows comments.

4. **Simplify the procedures for online applications.**

    Application administration is a known pain point for many firms. Too many companies have been juggling applications across several platforms, which has led to programs getting misplaced or, in some cases, disappearing completely.

Using an online application portal, Salesforce Experiences enables businesses to automate and simplify even the most complicated application procedures. Applicants can register on the portal, see calls for proposals, submit an application, and follow the application's progress. Additionally, the application portal can include a knowledge base where candidates can consult frequently asked questions, read pertinent articles, and communicate with one another.

Camp Harbor View

Every summer, Camp Harbor View (CHV) transforms the lives of one thousand young people and improves Boston by showing marginalized youngsters the possibilities of a future they might not have imagined. Through an eight-week summer camp and a year-round leadership academy that offers parent programs, career exploration, and academic support,

CHV offers unique experiences.

In 2018, Vera Solutions started collaborating with Camp Harbor View to put in place a powerful Salesforce camp administration system. The online application gateway, linked to the Camp Harbor View website, allows for the centralization of camper enrollment and applications. Through the portal, parents can manage their online camper applications, change contact details, and submit applications (which are based on Form Assembly).

The application system has allowed CHV to consolidate its sources of truth into a single central platform, replacing the twelve platforms that staff members had previously used. Now, the staff can send out bulk emails to potential applicants, guide them through the application process, and, if needed, follow up with campers' parents. CHV staff may now simply send enrollment or waitlist notices to hundreds of campers' parents at once, all with a single click during the enrollment process.

5. **Improve staff feedback loops to empower them.**

Today's multinational corporations are always trying to get more data-driven so they can make decisions that are more productive and efficient. Strong feedback loops are necessary for this, providing employees from headquarters to the field with the knowledge they need to effectively inform, enhance, and expand their jobs.

Although Experience Cloud is often associated with expanding your system's reach to external stakeholders, it also offers huge businesses an affordable means of democratizing data within their walls. Organizations may now finally break free from the one-way flow of data norms by utilizing a secure portal to give field personnel access to the most pertinent data and to move decision-makers closer to the source of truth regarding program impact.

International Population Services

A global nonprofit organization, Population Services International (PSI) is dedicated to promoting health-conscious behavior and ensuring that health products are reasonably priced. PSI uses Experience Cloud to centralize performance data and support local, national, and international decision-making for its hundreds of field sales representatives.

The Taro Works field service app and PSI's Salesforce system are integrated, allowing sales representatives to log sales transactions and distribution-related activities even when they're not online. Following the restoration of connectivity, the gathered data is automatically loaded into PSI's centralized Salesforce system. From there, international teams working in Social Enterprise, Finance, and Marketing can use PowerBI to analyze, visualize, and report on aggregated results and exchange product and stock-keeping unit spending across national borders.

6. **Connect and collaborate on common goals**

To tackle the most critical issues of the day, companies must collaborate more than in the past. However, companies far too frequently tackle these difficulties with fragmented approaches and lone efforts that are unable to deal with the issues at the scope at which they occur. Community-driven enterprises can establish crucial connections between entrepreneurs, practitioners, and organizations by utilizing Salesforce Experiences. This can create a forum for questioning, knowledge sharing, and encouraging group action towards shared objectives.

Impact Center

Impact Hub collaborates with businesses and institutions that prioritize social innovation. Building entrepreneurial communities for impact at scale is the mission of Impact Hub, one of the largest networks in the world, with over 100 Impact Hubs worldwide and over 16,000 members in 60 countries.

Experience Cloud has been used by Impact Hub since 2017 to promote communication and cooperation among its members worldwide. "Connecting with individuals engaged in comparable work worldwide is a desire shared by all," states Petr Skvaril, the Global Partnership Director at Impact Hub. In actuality, a lot of startups don't go beyond their surrounding area while tackling problems. We can enable more effective worldwide relationships using Salesforce. Impact Hub's "Global Community App," which was developed on Experience Cloud, has expanded to thousands of users in recent years.

Conclusion

We consider the plethora of tactics and insights that have emerged in front of us as we close this voyage through the world of Salesforce. The road to Salesforce mastery is paved with perseverance, never-ending study, and an uncompromising commitment to quality. The publications we've looked through offer a wealth of knowledge to assist you navigate the constantly changing world of consumer engagement, regardless of your experience level as a developer or as a burgeoning enthusiast for the Marketing Cloud. Keep in mind that your career is a canvas and that you are painting bright strokes onto your professional masterpiece with every skill you master and certification you obtain. Thus, seize the opportunities, commemorate the accomplishments, and allow your ideal Salesforce job to soar on the backs of proficiency and creativity.

www.ingramcontent.com/pod-product-compliance
Lightning Source LLC
Chambersburg PA
CBHW050245230526
45470CB00005B/2115